NOTHING [*poems*] IS FOR EVERYONE

EDEN PEARLSTEIN

Nothing Is for Everyone by Eden Pearlstein

A Deuteronomy Press Publication

Deuteronomy Press is a publisher of speculative books on spiritual themes. We are a home for writers and artists with unique visions of our inner and outer landscapes. In all written text, there is a remnant of the ineffable, a spark of transcendence. At Deuteronomy Press, we see creative expression as a sacred service—a way to create new worlds, and not merely to annotate our experience. When we make art, we tap into elemental wellsprings. These springs are a reminder of our origins; their murmuring is the song of our souls.

To contact Deuteronomy Press: hello@deuteronomy.com or write to Deuteronomy Press: PO Box 4, Afton, VA 22920
www.deuteronomy.com
Follow us on Instagram or Facebook @DeuteronomyPress
© 2024 Deuteronomy Press LLC
First edition, first printing

Cover design: Tom Haviv
Layout: Tom Haviv & Cory Rockliff
Typesetting: Cory Rockliff
Editor: Benjamin Bond
Manager of Operations: Noah Maxwell Flinkman

Nothing Is for Everyone

Distributed by Ayin Press via Publishers Group West, an Ingram brand
ISBN (paperback): 978-1-959586-02-9
ISBN (e-book): 978-1-959586-03-6
Library of Congress Control Number: 2023950947

Printed in the United States of America on acid-free paper

This book has been typeset in Adelle Sans, Interstate, Minion Pro, Sabon Next LT Pro and Secular One.

For Olam
who taught me
that "infinity is
not a number,
it's a word."

Praise for *Nothing Is for Everyone*

"One gets the sense from accompanying the wandering lines of this book that one has violated something ancient and sacred just by reading it. And yet, right there in the dimly lit room of the book's unfurling, the composer himself smiles seductively, through alchemical lines too fugitive for common sense—as if to encourage us to stray. So I did. I read it all up. And now I'm *lost*. The view has never been finer!"

—Bayo Akomolafe, author of *These Wilds Beyond Our Fences: Letters to My Daughter on Humanity's Search for Home*

In the tradition of holy trickster-poets like Christopher Smart, Rebbe Nachman of Breslav, and the great kabbalists, these poems knit together the realm of kaleidoscopic fantasy and the doughy academy of the body. Using language as a candle to illuminate his way, Pearlstein interrogates the boundaries between human and divine, carrying on an ancient tradition of midrashic commentary, unearthing something deep and true about our life on earth: "God's greenglasshouse / That dark fragile tower / Only built to fall."

—Alicia Jo Rabins, author of *Fruit Geode* and *Divinity School*

If prose tells a story, poetry pokes holes in the plot. Don't think! Imagine! Don't explain! Rupture! In this potent collection of poems, Eden Pearlstein lures us into a cavernous space of images: fire, shadow, love, womb, name, spark, prayer, desire, archetype, insanity. These poems don't let you rest, but as you continue to read, you no longer want to. When you are done you will be out of breath. But as you venture again to inhale, the air will be sweeter. More textured. More alive.

—Shaul Magid, author of *The Necessity of Exile: Essays from a Distance*

"Eden Pearlstein's *Nothing Is for Everyone* is soaked in the imagery of kabbalah and nondual consciousness—mystical and timeless, yet somehow relevant to walking down the street. The poems draw us in but never quite resolve into simple narrative (much like the world around us). There is something pointillist about these poems, something atomic that breaks down consciousness into its component parts, "every piece a puzzle unto itself." These careful and potent observations from a modern kabbalist's notebook offer a slant on Jewish theology that embraces the particular while dissolving into the cosmic; brilliantly directing us toward the nothing that is so deeply, specifically and gloriously—us.

—Rabbi Jill Hammer, author of *Undertorah: An Earth-Based Kabbalah of Dreams*

"From the impish, ecstatic wordplay embedded in the title, all the way to the alliterative Ars Poetica em-dashed into the final line, *Nothing Is for Everyone* is not just brimming with a deep sense of the music of language: better, perhaps, to say that it is tapped directly into language's musicvein. Mystical and melodic, weird and winking, reverent and rebellious, profane and profound, these poems are at once a yawp, a playground and a supplication."

—Moriel Rothman-Zecher, author of *Before All the World*

"In his soulfully singular voice, Eden Pearlstein keeps it light and playful, while remaining ever-mindful of the depths and paradoxes.

—Rodger Kamenetz, author of *The Missing Jew: Poems 1976-2022*

"In these rhythmic and mystery-laden poems that evoke both personal depth and vibrant soundings of the sacred, Eden Pearlstein draws forth the contours of a contemporary mythology that is at once earthy and existential, metaphysical and mundane. In *Nothing Is for Everyone*, Pearlstein emerges as a poet who weaves together mystical transcendence; the deep well of motifs and symbols of the Jewish tradition; and a surprisingly fresh music of the fragile and all-too-human soul."

—Eitan P. Fishbane, author of *The Art of Mystical Narrative: A Poetics of the Zohar*

With playful grace, Eden Pearlstein tugs at the essence of what makes life meaningful and what kindles spirit. From parenthood to the perspective of the soul to the paradox of being at home in exile, Pearlstein's poetry asks and answers the most foundational and far out questions at the heart of the human experience.

—Madison Margolin, author of *Exile and Ecstasy: Growing Up With Ram Dass and Coming of Age in the Jewish Psychedelic Underground*

Eden Pearlstein's *Nothing Is for Everyone* is a revelation. A master wordsmith of our generation, Pearlstein playfully provokes his readers to consider the beauty, the terror, and the absurdity of existence through his signature poetic mix of spoken word, deep hasidic storytelling, overflowing hilarity, and a refusal to let any particular sentence reach its naturally expected outcome. Buy this book today.

—-Joey Weisenberg, author of *The Torah of Music*

To read *Nothing Is for Everyone* is to gain access to a dynamic space where worlds collide—from family to philosophy, anarchism to esoterica. The multivocality of the text and many layers of meaning to be discovered in every line draw me back again and again. It may be true that Nothing Is for Everyone, but I believe that in this brilliant book everyone will find something that moves their heart, expands their mind, and speaks to their soul.

—Adina Allen, author of *The Place of All Possibility: Cultivating Creativity Through Ancient Jewish Wisdom*

These words gesture at the transcendent in almost secret ways: the hidden pun, the oblique reference, the *supernatural extra brilliant intelligent kindness of the soul.* But there is a deeper secret: that they are a gesture of the immanent, too, in their negative spaces, lacunae, and silences. That is when Eden Pearlstein persuades you that *Nothing Is for Everyone.*

—Jay Michaelson, author of *The Secret That Is Not a Secret: Ten Heretical Tales*

Introduction

■

In the beginning was poetry—at least in my own personal genesis.

At the tail end of a carnivalesque adolescence—blue hair at my bar mitzvah—poetry appeared like a Rimbaudian angel out of the fire of my life, opening new paths to previously imperceptible parallel universes.

It was through early encounters with poets like Bob Kaufman, D.A. Levy, Dianne di Prima, and Emily Dickinson that I first began to actively explore the realms of memory and myth, ritual and art, music and magick, protest and provocation. Buber, Benjamin, Borges, and Nachman of Breslov came later, adding dimension and depth.

From Free Jazz to Freestyle, Qawwali to Concrete, it was through poetry that I first heard spirit speak—to me and to the world—and so began to listen, and respond. What most often resulted was a kind of trance/scription of fleeting moments and mindstates—phenomenological sheet music.

Poetry turned me on—sensitizing me to more deeply notice and appreciate, challenging me to more faithfully render and distill. And as a teeth-grinding tweeker once told me on a dirty couch after his roommate handed me my first book of anarcho-occult philosophy: *once you're on the path, you can never get off.*

■ ■

Over the past two decades, I have dedicated much of my creative energy to cultivating a career as a performing artist and trickster-teacher of Jewish text, thought, and practice. At the same time, I remained engaged in various book-works—helping to develop, write, and edit over forty volumes of contemporary Kabbalah, and co-founding an artist-run publishing house and production studio, Ayin Press.

However—aside from a few years in high school when I read my poems every Thursday night at a small club in south Phoenix eating homemade cinnamon buns baked by our heavenly host who everyone called "Big Mama"—my poetry has remained an almost entirely private practice; a hermetic art in every sense of the word pursued *lishmah*, as they say, for its own sake.

And yet, in spite (and because) of such seclusion, my poetry—which has always been the foundation of both my creative and spiritual life—has continued to flourish and nourish me like an ever-evolving species of flora that grows better by the light of the moon; always written with a reader in mind, yet, perpetually kept in the dark—until now.

■ ■ ■

The poems included in this volume are culled from the last twenty-five years of clandestine poetic activity—from the night of my seventeenth birthday when I wrote my first verse in a silver spiral-bound notebook with a UFO on the cover, to the middle of a charred wood typing this introduction on a Macbook with the first patches of silver popping up like mushrooms in my beard at age forty-two.

Aphoristic, lyrical, critical, and playful—each of these poems is an expression of my own desire to enact a kind of secular heiros gamos; reconciling Sontag's "erotics of art" with a post-rabbinic slapstick sense of hermeneutical aesthetics. Torah, Tarot, Kabbalah, and many other models, maps, and methods have been imbibed and employed liberally throughout.

Far from a fawning fanaticism for any particular storyline or set of beliefs, my lettristic practice has only led me to further investigate the limits of the alphabet—its ability to convey and connect, as well as to confuse and corrupt.

■ ■ ■ ■

When words become weapons, language itself is the prison we must break out of. Not to leave it all behind—as if that were even possible—but to carry it, and ourselves along with it, forward or backward or both, out of our semiotic shackles, back into living presence.

From the enchantment of the garden, where the first human gives names to all of the animals, to the iconoclasm of the exodus, where G-d Herself rejects the confinement of static identification, *Nothing Is for Everyone* is a psycho-poetic journey along the fine lines between word and world.

A series of. Letters both. To and from. Thoughts—not ideas.

stranded in paradise

escape/isms

Poetry makes nothing happen 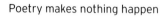 **Auden**

This does not mean nothing **Rimbaud**

stranded

in paradise

Jewish Geography (Tikkun HaShem)

Everyone knows
Before a child is
Born an angel
In the womb
Lights a candle
Above their head
And teaches them
The entire Torah.

On the doorstep
Of this world
The angel taps
The child above
Their lip causing
Them to forget
And learn it
All over again

On their own.

I am not
Ashamed to
Admit that
I have
Often wondered what
In the world
This means or
Why it matters;

And so late one
Night perplexed
I was moved
To press my ear
Against my
Sleeping wife's
Breast—and this is
What I heard:

Tiny sun
Curious star

I want to tell you
The story of
Your name

But first you must
Know that a name
Is not only a name

A name is a map
A name is a seed
A name is a path
A name is a deed
                        Yet to be done

In the middle of the great dream
There is a hidden garden
Where names grow on trees

The ancient one sang a secret song
To the earth and called forth the first
Name in honor of our verdant mother

Faithfully this name became
Became this fateful name

Until one day they ate a name
Off a branch of the name
That had been named by The Name

She was a planet
Pocketing names

He was a tangent
Toppling names

We were all grain
Scattered names in the wind

And so the world
Filled with names

Until we all became
A single name—

Peace

—the purpose
Of all of the names

And then we woke up

Here Goes Nothing

"Stranded in paradise,"
 she muttered to herself.
"Be home by exile!"
 he called out across an empty plain.

Face pressed flush against
White wall wailing within
God's greenglasshouse

That dark fragile tower
Only built to fall—

Arrive.
      Arrange.
           Arcana.
           The image
      That yearns
To be heard.

Words are wounds licked deeper
So slowly science starts to sing

The esoteric art
Of accidental enlightenment

Whatever is—what was necessary
However hopelessly—hopefully helpfully

Eight Days After Eternity

א

life begins kissing
the result of a need

suspension of disbelief
and there you are

back in the garden
with nothing to lose

can you explain
the balance of

the universe without
using your heart

ב

welcome to the
garden of paradox

the tunnel
at the end

of the light
trust yourself

you are an
ancestor

ג

moving with
unhindered

maniacal jerks
and spasms

we descend again
and then—

driven by desire upward
shoot towards

the surface
of our destiny

leaving behind
only a path

of dust and
shed skin

ד

pavement before me
frozen black river

streetlights reflecting
like stars

going nowhere
being everywhere

spiritual activism
political mysticism

outlaw redemption
freedom is a lit match

burning books
history is dead

story of my life
without living

ה
there really is
something out there

beyond the horizon
it will bury you

beneath what you
thought was real

eyes rolled back
in the mirror looking

for a friend
welcome to wherever you are

ו
this funny old
world of ours

don't tell
anyone

but I think
we're all asleep

dreaming of
a better place

somewhere
soft and warm

tender fire alive
within us all

ד
if the sculptor
never ceases

we are left with
nothing but dust

ח
collective circumcision
carving of the tribe
sacrifice identity
the night my ego died

punish and reward the state
paradox is fact and fake

feed on greed and fear and hate
either/or make no mistake

mother doesn't want you
father's far from home
amputated consciousness
collage of flesh and bone

Squatters' Rites

I

I don't
belong
here

any more
or less
than
      you do.

We are all
bad astronauts
crash-landed in

paradise
clutching our
star-charts,

cursing
and kicking up
dust—

II

The world
was created
31 years ago

At the
exact
moment

I shit
my pants
on purpose;

A curious
cocktail
composed

Of equal parts
shame and
relief—

I think
they call it
being human.

III

The word
means nothing
if anything

Is everything.
The numbers
don't add up.

Still the music
sounds so
sacred

Sensual
surreal
or something

Suggesting that
it all comes down
to this:

For God's sake
make things
more beautiful

Than they were
before you got
here—then

Vanish.
Anything else is
trespassing.

Ode on a Grecian Urinal

All poetry is Promethean—*Great artists steal!*
Don't be so complex, Oedipus.
Won't that Sphinx just come to the table with the rest of us?

Wet leaves. Worn shoes. Burnt wood.
Bright. Windy. Ocean. Early.
Fingertips still smell like cigarettes.

Small face, turned upward, and in that moment
The earth really does revolve around my son—
Infinitesimal point of inconceivable gravity o love

A dream is more than what you feel inside the dream
A dream is more than what you see inside the dream
Poems are pebbles that you hold inside the dream

They skip on the surface
Then sink to the depths

Unbinding Isaac

More than a strut, it
was offensive, with telos,
my grandfather's gait.

"Walk, about one-and-
a-half times normal speed, and
swing your arms like this!

Five miles a day—
more if you can make it." His
only exercise

Imposing. Hope not
practical. Money worth more
than hugs—so he hopes.

First time he said "I
love you," outside hospice. "You're
next—to last—in line."

No pressure. First crack
in the shell of male bondage—
Isaac's sweet revenge:

"The most important thing
is that you are happy."
Thank God for that ram.

Who Is Speaking and Why

I am not a great man—
I am a psychoactive toad
Here to remind king David,
A truly great man, that I
Sing more praises than he.

I am not a self-important leader—
I am a snarky rooster
Shadow-boxing and serenading
The sun as it rises and shines,
You hope, on your good side.

I am no falling-star-struck celebrity—
I am a stoned meteorologist
Blissed out on swirling digital cloud
Formations forgetting that I'm live on
Late night tv telling myself it's all going to be ok.

I am not important, nor do I aspire to be.
I am neither inspiring, nor informative.
I am here. Silent. Staring. I see you.
I hear you. I love you. And I don't believe you.

It will all remain the same. Nothing will have
Changed. That will be the only difference.

What Philosophy Feels Like

I

Slant light passing through a pinhole
Casting shadows across a screen
Mounted on a cave wall preserved
In a wax museum replica of a brain
In a jar on the side of a road going
Nowhere

II

Whose tears fall
From the eyes of existence

In the dawn of awareness
something is lost

     ayeka

I
  am
    always
      only
      every
    where
  are
You

     hineni

III

I was buried in manuscripts
        during my fossil nap.
The walls are high and slippery.

My soul is bruised from
        obsolete attempts to scale the
Sneering madness of the bricks.

I wander, stumble, trip, float and crawl
        down the aisle towards the ultimate
Question—whatever it is—I do

IV

The perfection
of the moment
Hit me

As I laughed
At the hopelessness
of our fate

■

The hopelessness
of our fate
Punked me

As I wept
At the perfection
of the moment

V

All stars sing the
Secret name in silence while we
Read ourselves to sleep

Remember this: deep
As the heart is, without lips
There is no kiss—

VI

THIS

Today's Forecast (Weather or Not)

Nothing bores the ordinary man more than the cosmos. Hence, for him, the deepest connection between weather and boredom ... Nothing is more characteristic than that precisely this most intimate and mysterious affair, the working of the weather on humans, should have become the theme of their emptiest chatter.

Walter Benjamin

What remains of a beach
The sound of waves
        Crashing

What remains of this life
O pocketful of
        Sand

A/lone man sits on the edge of a
Crumbling pier   breathing in
The vast wreckage   wondering
Why   he is no longer
        Moved

Faint taste of salt on cracked lips
        Blink

Another perfect picture
Taken by the
        Moon

Old friends talk late
Searching for lost sparks

Anything to remind them
Of the world they left behind

A storm gathers overhead
Hijacking every conversation

And after that
Another one

Transcribing the Wind

Jazz—listen to it at your own risk.
Jazz, don't listen to it at your own risk.

Bob Kaufman

I

spiderfingers and lotuseyes
pluck it quick and hard, keeping
time in relative obscurity

perception comes crashing in
on the spontaneous crest
of a swinging wave

and is sent exploding
back in the mouth
of a screaming tulip

jazz is
and
that is
all

moon beams
and this
is enough

in a moment of
religious city
silence

a cymbal is tossed
from the heavens
to grace the troubled brow
of the next martyr

people always love
        musicians—
        poets
just talk loud

II

stumbling down *Solitudes*
Crowded with Loneliness
confused by the clarity

threads of absolute
        abandon
decorate the terrace
        overlooking
reveries of consciousness
        devoid
of what could have been

a woeful moan
shuffles home

with a saxophone
strapped to her back

sending out sound waves

sharper than steel

to obliterate the gripping vines
of another chance

sparks announce the fusion
of lips and brass

III

if the Word is God,
then what is music
—that thing we all need

a way to be together
that doesn't use or break
but works and plays well
with and for others

a moment ago this was just
a sad room full of empty
algorithms, we were only what
we had been—bought or sold

but the music changed all that
made the light look different
ennobled us blessed us brought us
out of our own image unafraid

of the night

Doulas of the Dawn
(in the Dark Light of the Zohar)

Day breaks. The Night has conceived.

Edmond Jabès

we stand alone
together in awe
ready to receive

the gifts borne
and bestowed by
the doe at dawn

we are bound
by Her love
in a circle

defined by
the snake
of our spine

She arrives—no,
appears without us
even noticing how

suddenly She is just
there—no,
here

we sing softly
as She screams
silently, giving entirely

of what She
has—no,
of what She is

we are filled too
overflowing the
basis of blessing

basking in the
color of silence

She is beaming
She is bursting
She is bleeding
She is birthing

first light—then
day—call it good
after words—we
are what—remains

words/myth

The palace stands inside a square that has been long deserted
With a sign slung from the gate on purpose poorly worded

written in a cryptic script
familiar and strange
welcoming or menacing
depending on the sage

For those inclined to take the time to scale the outer wall
A snake awaits inside the gate to make sure that they fall

for no one ever learned to walk
without their share of spills
and every moth must crash and burn
to learn how fire feels

The sights and smells seduce the soul to sing the world awake
Which brings the rain upon the plains so parched and out of place

four rivers flow out from the garden
grows who knows the outcome
of the seed inside the fruit
that floats above the fountain

Two trees in one unspoken tongue, leaves looking for a sign
A point a line a time to turn from grapes of wrath to wine

Holy broken tears of joy douse the angel's ire
Whose jealousy is sharp as swords forged in holy fire

a sudden kiss upon the lips
switch/blades of grass to words
a drop of dew green drunk on blue
a conference of the birds

a school of fish a troop a tryst
a spoof a game of chance
a thousand-letter leap of faith
across the page we dance

A child sits upon the throne whose feet don't reach the ground
Leaving it up to the help to find the fallen crown

we search and sweep, we curse and weep
the world is upside down
the holy thief plays hide and seek
knows nothing never now

G-d creates *yesh me'ayin*, something from nothing.

It is our task to create *ayin me'yesh*, nothing from something.

Magid of Mezritch

escape/

isms

Musick in Theory and Practice

Pianos provide up to 88 keys
just to open one very small door,
which is locked on both sides and guarded by
angels wielding their fiery swords.
But if you can make it through all of the
obstacles and you still want to come in,
the only thing left is to tickle the
ivories up close and under their

chin.

The gates have been closed for so long it shows
their hinges have started to rust,
there's piles of bones from the other souls
whose dreams have turned into dust.
While patiently waiting and perfectly
playing their songs like it was a recital,
they had forgotten the door they were
knocking on led to a big tent

revival.

There was a man without any hands who
would stand on the side and just listen
to all of the fans: "This must be a scam!
The door's jammed, it won't budge a smidgen!"
But he had a plan to sit at the grand
and pretend that he was a musician—
just for a moment before someone
noticed he stealthily took his position.

And that's when it happened, the laughin and
clappin and all of the hootin' and hollerin'—
the man with no hands at the foot of the
grand in a trance as he brought up his offering.
He trembled and shivered and stared at the
instrument, ignorant but with devotion.
He dropped to his knees, banged his head on the
keys, and with that the door finally

opened.

in the museum of faith
my rebbe is an art thief

I myself will exhibit nothing.

Marcel Duchamp

Stick Figures of Speech

This whole thing rubs me the wrong way
They're just stroking your ego
I have an abrasive personality
She's a bit prickly
He has a magic touch
That's my personal signature
Let's be in contact
Sometimes life is hard
Don't be such a softie
It's a delicate matter
That's heavy
You're a real lightweight
This situation requires kid-gloves
Touchy, touchy
I've got thick skin
You've lost your grip
Beauty is only skin-deep
The darkness was tangible
And thus, shall ye cleave to the Lord
That gave me goosebumps
Very tactfully rendered
How are you feeling
I just need something to hold onto
My Rock and my Redeemer
This teaching is a touchstone
I can't quite put my finger on it
You should keep your distance
I'll reach out tomorrow

I feel very held right now
It's no skin off my back
Language touches without touching

The Fiftieth Gate

The young rabbi sits
The young rabbi learns
The young rabbi twists
The young rabbi turns

Is turned
        Détourned
Returns
Concerned

The old rabbi speaks
The old rabbi stares
The old rabbi weeps
The old rabbi's tears

Whet the page where
Fire and water kiss

The earth
        A book

Of letters
        Let her
        Let there
Be light

Clear
        Sight:

Gates within gates
In closing they open
Shapes within shapes
In folding they function

The world awaits

unpunctuated

shorts

I

the painter sits
staring struck
dumb at the empty
canvas.

Still Life with Cezanne
signed, Orange '08.

II

the wind questions:
"i hear you are a master of the way"

the water answers:
"oh no, i am but a poor student"

III

man has vision of
god on deathbed says:
"where you been
all my life?"

IV

israelites wandered through
central park forty years
before they entered the
upper west side

V

an old blind jew,
who had seen a thing or two,
once said to their grandchild:
"it's better to be smart than to be happy."

the child, surprised,
lovingly replied:
"if you're so smart,
then why aren't you happy?"

VI

crickets:

Confessions of a Clarinet

Saxophones are sexier
Trumpets more iconic
Flutes are so fanciful—
        almost folkloric.

Then there's me, a little old
Licorice stick. At fifteen Yitzy would
Sneak out the yawning windows of
Davenport during the Depression
Clutching me carelessly in his sweaty left palm,
Drunk on the sweet wine of youth with no future.

Who could see such a war coming
That would wipe out whole genres
Leaving lonely instruments like me
Alive with no one left to listen.

One glass eye and one thousand-yard stare later,
Mr. Pearlstein didn't play no more.
He purchased and persuaded and imposed
His strict music on whoever would listen—
And if not, he would
Make you listen.

But I was the funny bone in his boarded up closet
Full of prewar skeletons—brilliant
Neurotic conductor of shrill laughter
Heard now only at Jewish mothers' weddings
Or fetish festivals of thee olde fatherland;

                Either way—the kids don't get it.

Puzzling

Big picture
       Broken open
       Cracked
Right down
The center
       Gives way
       Shatters myths
And mirrors
       Scatters
Seeds of light

Pixelating
       Pangea
       Poetry is
Pointillism
Taken personally
       Consciousness
       Itself
A kind of
       Continental
Drift

Whose hand
Moves mountains
Carves rivers
Paints faces
Gets frustrated
Forgets to
Finish walks

Away leaves
Sparks strewn
About free
Will floating
Falling fending
For ourselves

Faith feels
Like this

Putting things
Together—Alone

Every piece
A puzzle
Unto itself

esc/art

In order to become engaged,
art first had to learn betrayal.

Boris Groys

i'm working on becoming
       invisible.

disappearance is
       more than an act;

for shamans, spies, and snitches—
       it's initiation.

an artist is a thief who
       longs to be caught;

reissuing a limited run
       of fine fingerprints.

winning is for
       losers.

fame is fake
       for real.

poetry is the perfect
       crime—

nothing is for everyone

A Futility Worth Facing

I can only answer that if one is faithful enough, constant enough, the
analysis will induce the synthesis, the poet will come home: he will
have tramped the whole road, he will have seen. By taking the universe
apart he will have reintegrated it with his own vitality; and it is this
reintegrated universe that will in turn possess him and give him rest.
If this voyage reveals a futility, it is a futility worth facing.

Laura Riding

Brittle branches scratch
Cracked skin of sky

Detached

A leaf
Falls

Spin
Hold
Release

Aloof
Stars

Breathe light
Back to those
Brittle branches

And sing

Prayer: an Unofficial Biography

Robes
Bells
Strings
Shells
Skin
        Smells
        Secret
Spells

Stone
Metal
Fire
Water
Music
Magic
Letters
        Laughing
            Sighing
                Soaring

Spreading their wings
To escape from the scroll

Leaves
        Fallen
Fruits
        Forbidden
Flowers
        Forgotten

                    So
                    Fragile
          Left
                    Pressed
          Between
Breasts
          Before
Books
          Burned
All
Those
Eyes
          In the forest

                    So dark
          At night
          Where
Gazelles
          Roam
          Free
          From
Desire
          Hidden
                    Deeper
                    Higher
Falcon's
Talons
Snake
          or
Spider

Prey

              Prays
              Digs
Dirt
              Works
Earth
              Hurts
Heart
              Heals
Head
Hands
              Hold

Keys to the
Castle in a
Clearing of trees

Sky
              Swallows
Sound
              Black
Light
              Blue
Breath
              Bound
              Held
              Back
              Between
Worlds
              Beyond
Words
              Ground
              Down

Gates
      Locked
      Guarded
Garden
      Stolen
      Starving
Artist
      Sharpen
Swords
Verse
Shovels

      Strike
Bone
Silence
      Shown
Nothing
      Known
      Grown
      So
      Beautiful
I
      Surrender
            Undelivered

      Return
      To
Sender

Home in Exile

Had I but one familiar sun
What need would I have runes?

I'd ply the sky so high and dry
And return right at noon.

But that has not my chosen lot
Been from day one or two,

My orbit snakes in figure eights
Face painted on the moon.

Fuzzy logic
Chaos magic
Quantum poetics.

Everything is
A big deal for
The God of small things.

Torah is a thesaurus
With infinite entries
For only one Word.

With this many
Windows, why have
Walls at all?

Without a strong
Circumference

The center just can't hold.

Artist meets Abacus;
Awareness drawn
And quartered—

The opposite of
Attention Deficit
Disorder.

My interest rates
Are through the roof.

Leaving the temple in ruins
Is good for business,

Attracting more pilgrims in pieces
Than standing still intact;

An embarrassment
Of riches.

No admission
Free of charge

Jungian Slips

An unconscious symbol is lived but not perceived.

Edward Edinger

po-mo got fomo
and came back
from the future

to lay bricks and
blame with the
rest of us

the new agnostics
believe in Netflix
but can't decide
what to watch

the panopticon has
become too fetishized
to fulfill its function
any longer—or harder

the text
strikes back
to interpret
the reader

is that a cigar
putting an old
man to shame

or did I just
slip and step in
someone else's name?

sub/text

i am convincing you
are convinced i have
read more books than
you or better combinations
of just the right
books i have understood
things in ways you
never could unless I
told you i am
putting my thoughts in
your head right now
so you can feel
like they are yours

i am giving myself
to you and all
i ask in return
is that you
[fill in the blank]

hear/say

Our vocation is to be nothing.

Fernando Pessoa

How hard it is to forget
All that one has heard
But that is what it takes for one
To sing a single word

The experts and the scholars all
Protest, "that's incorrect!"
While critics fidget with their flies
The egg has fled the nest

Philosophers and philologues
In haste they taint the trace
With dervish dance or wordless chant
The purists paint their face

Economists and activists
All clamor for a claim
Seeking to enlist the wind
To fan their faction's flames

As rabbis priests monks and imams
Transform light to law
Fools and children never fail
To answer Raven's call:

Sunset tastes like strawberry
Soaked in moonshine memory
So fill your cup and lift it up
O purple—perfume—poetry

I have just completed a very long descent
into nothingness....I never put an end
to my work, which is the Magnum Opus,
such as the Great Work was called by
our ancestors, the alchemists.

Stéphane Mallarmé

Notes

xvi Poetry makes nothing happen Auden, "In Memory of W.B. Yeats."

xvi This does not mean nothing Rimbaud, "Letter to George Izambard, May 13, 1871."

2 Jewish Geography A popular name-game played when Jews meet each other for the first time and try to identify people they know in common. Typically, it goes something like this: "You're from [insert name of city here]? Do you know [insert person's name here]?" Both the game and the concept are Jewish-specific examples of the "six degrees of separation" theory proposed by Hungarian writer Frigyes Karinthy in 1929 and the "small world phenomenon" hypothesized by social scientist Stanley Milgram in 1967. While the accuracy of these theories has been questioned by some, this name-game has become something of an informal social custom in the Jewish community, and it is often surprisingly easy for strangers who play it to discover mutual acquaintances and establish instant context and connection.

2 Tikkun HaShem A play on the popular Jewish phrase *Tikkun Olam*, which means "fixing the world." In Hebrew, *HaShem* literally translates as "The Name," and is used to refer to G-d, whose name cannot be pronounced. *Tikkun HaShem* then literally translates as "Fixing The Name." I have previously introduced the phrase *Tikkun Adam* (fixing the human) to refer to the work we must do on ourselves in order to be the change we want to see in the world. As I have continued reflecting, it seems clear to me that we inevitably take on the forms and characteristics that we project onto the Divine (or its absence)—we were "created in [their] image" after all. Therefore, in order to achieve desired change in the world, we must work on our *midot* (psycho-emotional character attributes) as well as on our *shemot* (conceptions/names for G-d or Ultimate Reality). The world is not the problem, we are. *It should be noted that according to Jewish tradition, peace is both the means and the end of this fixing. As it says in the Mishna (Masechet Oktzin, third chapter): *G-d did not find a vessel for blessing other than peace;* and as we learn in the Zohar (Vayikra 23): *G-d is peace, G-d's name is peace, and everything is connected in peace.*

17 *Ayeka* Literally translates as "Where are you?" Biblically, *Ayeka* is considered the primary existential question. We hear it from G-d inquiring after Adam and Eve following their eating from the Tree of Knowledge in the garden. This is the Divine *Ayeka*, which echoes within each of us at all times, calling us into presence. Conversely, we hear the pained question from the prophet Jeremiah, in the title of his famous book of Lamentations. This is the Human *Ayeka*, calling forth G-d from out of the void in moments of suffering, doubt, and destruction.

17 *Hineni* Literally translates as "Here I am." Biblically, this is considered the optimal answer to the existential question, *Ayeka?* It communicates radical presence and a sense of responsibility, for others as well as for oneself.

20 Nothing bores the ordinary man more than the cosmos… Walter Benjamin, *The Arcades Project*.

22 Jazz—listen to it at your own risk "War Memoir: Jazz, Don't Listen To It At Your Own Risk" by Robert Kaufman, from THE ANCIENT RAIN, copyright ©1981 by Bob Kaufman. Reprinted by permission of New Directions Publishing Corp.

22 Jazz, don't listen to it at your own risk Bob Kaufman, excerpt from "O-Jazz" from Cranial Guitar: Selected Poems. Copyright © 1996 by Eileen Kaufman. Reprinted with the permission of The Permissions Company, LLC. on behalf of Coffee House Press, www.coffeehousepress.org.

23 Solitudes Crowded with Loneliness *Solitudes Crowded with Loneliness,* book by Bob Kaufman.

25 Day breaks. The Night has conceived. Edmond Jabès, *The Book of Questions: Volume One.*

30 G-d creates *yesh me'ayin*, something from nothing... Magid of Mezritch, as quoted by his son Avraham Ha-Malach in *Chesed l'Avraham.*

34 I myself will exhibit nothing Marcel Duchamp, "Letter to Walter Arensberg, November 8, 1918."

45 In order to become engaged, art first had to learn betrayal Boris Groys, *Logic of the Collection.*

46 I can only answer that if one is faithful enough, constant enough... Laura Riding, "A Prophecy or a Plea."

53 An unconscious symbol is lived but not perceived Edward Edinger, *Ego and Archetype.*

56 Our vocation is to be nothing Fernando Pessoa, *Book of Disquiet.*

59 I have just completed a very long descent into nothingness... Stéphane Mallarmé, as quoted in *Alchemist of the Avant Garde,* by John Moffitt.

Acknowledgments

I have often referred to myself as a chronic collaborator. Whether I am working on music, film, design, publishing, learning, or teaching—it is the magic that emerges between two or more people in process that really ignites and excites me. Maybe that is why it has taken me so long to share my poetry with a wider audience; it has been, for the most part, a practice of creative *hitbodedut*, a meditative, even prayerful, form of secluded expression (or expressive seclusion).

Of course, that is not entirely accurate. When are we ever truly alone? There is no vacuum within which any of us exist purely independent from any relationship or influence. And so with that in mind, I would like to acknowledge a small handful of people who have contributed to, impacted, informed, inspired, challenged,and blessed my being and doing throughout the years:

My parents Suzan and Lynn Pearlstein, without whom I would not exist, in more ways than one; my wife Chani Trugman—my rock, ocean, sky, and beyond; our crazy/wonderful children Olam and Raziel, who have blessed us with so much joy, responsibility, and love beyond measure; my sister/hero and brother-in-love Jordan Pearlstein and James Herman; my brother Cannupa Hanska Luger, with whom I began this journey so many years ago; Ginger Dunnill; Adam Segula Sher, with whom I endlessly wander in wonder; Megan Sher; Kelly Lydick, who opened the door; Brianna Connell, who led me through it; Douglas Mackar, who cut the apple and licked the knife; Owen Taylor, who jumped from behind the turntables, bounced a heckler, and made it back to scratch the chorus; Zack Smith; Paul Schrag; who put me on the path and never left my side; Gabriel Bey Khan; the green man; Ceano Chicharron; the big dude in the back of the club with the basket of dates; Smoke, a heart in the shape of a human; James and Rusty Ridenour, keepers of the purple sword; Poopy Mouth Amy; Adar; AKA; XP; Compost; Glimpse; Marcus and Kissel; OSF; DDS; Lisa David; Jim and Toby Shulruff; Rabbi Seth Goldstein; Elizabeth Rene; Scoot Mecca; Calvin Johnson; Erez Safar; Mike Horowitz; Pickster Uno; Drunken Immortals; Shadow Guardians; Shir Yaakov, who sang my soul awake; Basya Schechter, who brought me into the palace of song; Dan and Ris Sieradski; Caural; Nomy Lamm; Gershon Winkler; Reb Zalman Schachter Shalomi, from whom I learned so much in such a short amount of time; Shaul Magid; Jill Hammer; Jay Michaelson; Amichai Lau Lavie; Rabbi Dovber and Rochie Pinson; my father- and mother-in-spirit Avraham Arieh and Rachel Trugman; Kathy Whitman, my mother from another brother; my uncle John and aunt Jody, definitely two of the thirty-six; Jamie Saft; Jon Madof; Papa Jube; Omar Akbar; Tom Haviv, who opened the eye in my palm; Penina Eilberg-Schwartz; Robin Margolis; Zahar Vaks; Gregory Welker; Jorian Polis Schutz, a true Ba'al Beha'alotecha; Ben Bond; Moshe Novakoff; Anna and Naf Hanua; Caren and Arthur Fried; Joanna Herman; Mr. Peterson; Mr. Miller; Madame Mousseau, Christine Marsh; Susan Preciso; and Craig Carlson, who blew smoke into the eyes of the dragon so I could get away.

to all the dead poets, and those not yet born—THANK YOU

Eden Pearlstein is a poet, performer, chronic collaborator, and cofounder of Ayin Press. Over the past two decades he has created an eclectic portfolio of audio, visual, textual, and curatorial works and projects. Eden is the coauthor and coeditor of the chapbooks *In/Flux: On Influence, Inspiration, Transmission, and Transformation; Taste and See: A Psychedelic Pesach Companion; Indwelling: An Earth-Based Sukkot Companion*; and the art book *Speechless* (with Cannupa Hanska Luger). Eden lives in Philadelphia with his wife and two children. *Nothing Is for Everyone* is Eden's first book-length publication.

www.edenpearlstein.com